ISBN: 0-87973-379-9 Casebound
ISBN: 0-87973-359-4 Paperbound

Library of Congress Catalog Card Number: 78-56878

Published, printed and bound by
Our Sunday Visitor, Inc.
Noll Plaza
Huntington, Indiana 46750

When God LISTENS

BY JOAN LOWERY NIXON

ILLUSTRATED BY JAMES McILRATH

Our Sunday Visitor, Inc.
Huntington, Indiana 46750

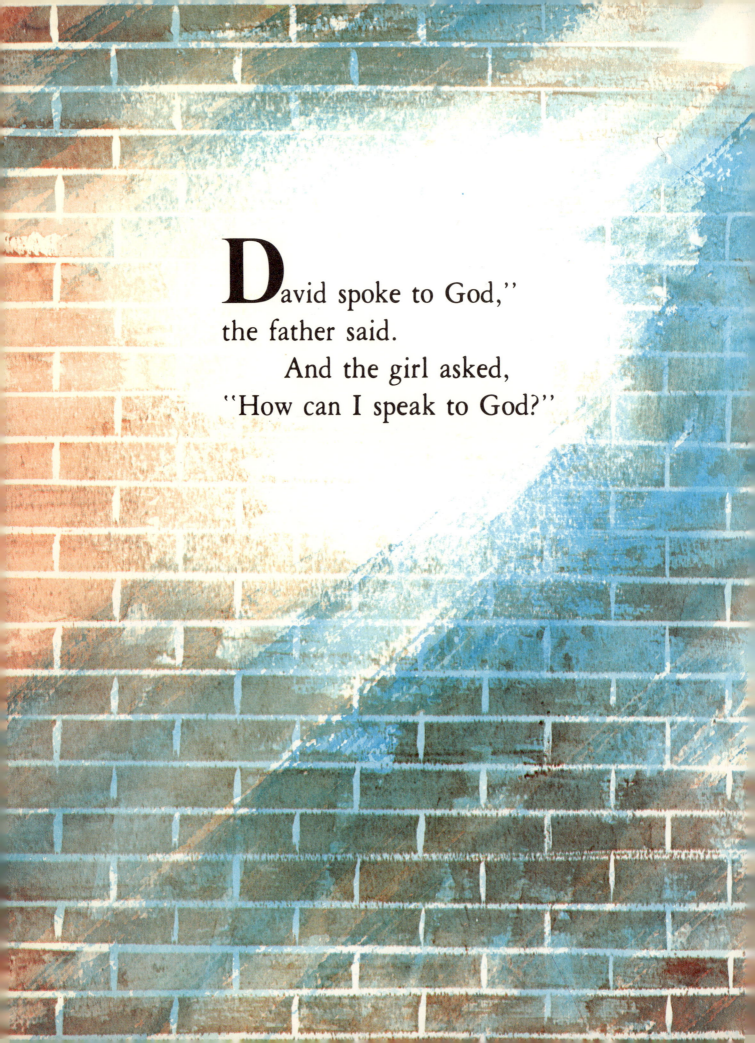

David spoke to God,"
the father said.
    And the girl asked,
"How can I speak to God?"

He held open the heavy door of
the apartment house, and she
skipped under his arm.
The summer sun slid warmly
over her arms and shoulders as
she reached up to hold
her father's hand.

A woman was laughing in an apartment across the street, the happy notes floating through the open window like sparks of bright light. They made the girl and her father laugh too.

Down on the sidewalk
a small boy tripped and
began to wail. His older
sister scooped him into her
arms, kissing his chubby neck
and murmuring, "It's all right
now. The hurt
will go
away."

David gave praise to God," the father said.

And the girl asked, "How can I give praise to God?"

At the corner a flower vendor held out a small blossom to the girl.

"For you," he said. "Because it's such a beautiful day!"

They entered a bakery, and the cinnamon-sugar smells curled around them. "A loaf of wheat bread, please," the father said.

The plump woman
behind the counter nodded
and smiled, the loose strands of
gray hair bouncing behind her
ears. She handed a chocolate
cookie to the girl.

"Because you're such a
good girl," she said.

Past the window
two boys ran,
throwing a ball
and shouting
for joy.

The girl and her father
walked back into the sunshine.
The girl brushed the last
of the chocolate cookie crumbs
from her mouth.

"David sang his praises to God,"
the father said.

And the girl asked,
"How can I sing praises
to God too?"

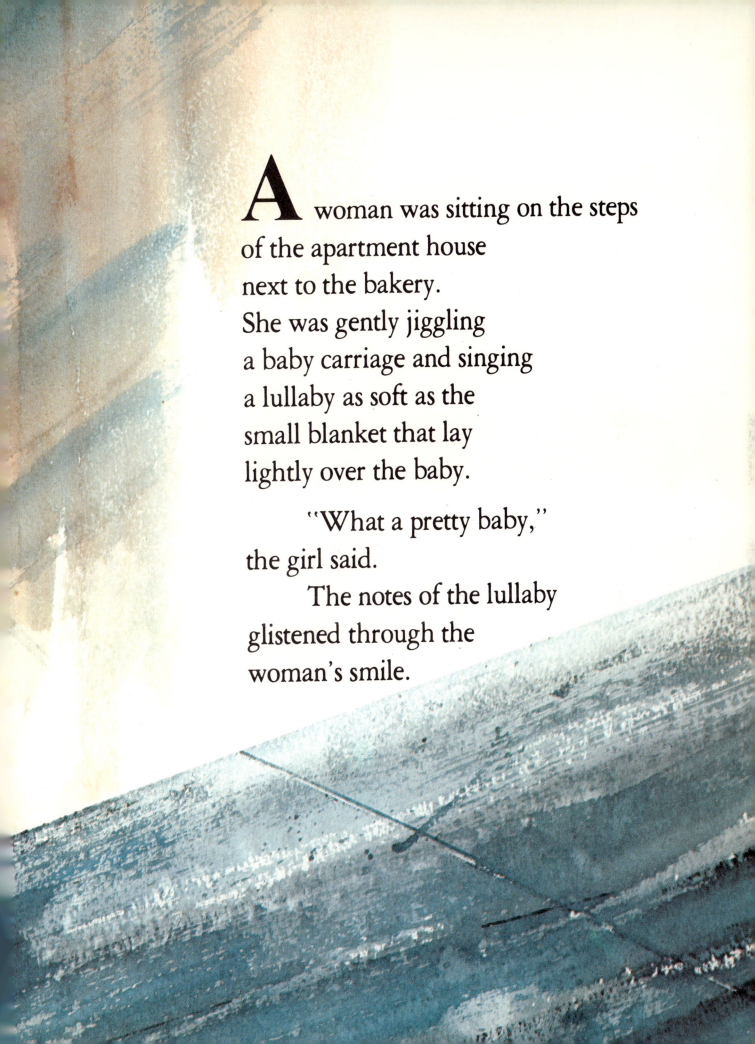

A woman was sitting on the steps
of the apartment house
next to the bakery.
She was gently jiggling
a baby carriage and singing
a lullaby as soft as the
small blanket that lay
lightly over the baby.

  "What a pretty baby,"
the girl said.
  The notes of the lullaby
glistened through the
woman's smile.

Upstairs, through the window
of a vocal teacher's apartment,
they could hear the tinny chords
of a piano, and a clear voice
that trilled up and down the scale.

"Beautiful! Beautiful!
Now, once again," came the deep,
encouraging voice of the teacher.

long the sidewalk skipped
two girls, their clasped hands
swinging in wide arcs.
At the top of their lungs
they were singing,
"Follow the yellow brick road . . .
Follow the yellow brick road . . ."

As they reached the girl,
they grasped her hands,
swung her around in a
circle of giggles, and
left, still singing,
"Follow the yellow
brick road . . ."

Sometimes David spoke to God to tell him he was sorry for what he had done," the father said.

And the girl asked, "How can I tell God when I am sorry?"

A woman stepped from a nearby doorway, her handbag over one arm, her string shopping bag

over the other. A boy ran after her, hugged her around the waist and said, "I'm sorry, Mama. I'm sorry I said that."

She stopped, bent down and kissed him. "I love you," she said. He began to smile. "I love you too."

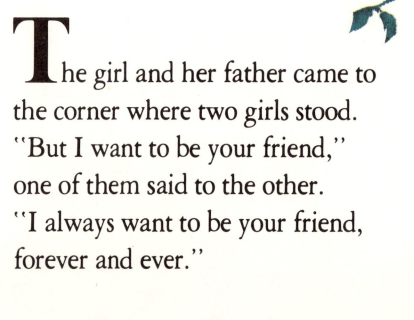

The girl and her father came to
the corner where two girls stood.
"But I want to be your friend,"
one of them said to the other.
"I always want to be your friend,
forever and ever."

"You do?" The second girl rubbed
a tear from her cheek. "Okay!
I'll race you to the park!"
The two girls dashed down the
sidewalk, their laughter trailing
behind them like bright banners.

The girl put her hand into her father's hand. They turned the corner, crossed the street, and walked into the park.

"When David spoke to God, it was in words of love," the father said.

And the girl said, "But that was a long time ago. How can I talk to God in words of love now?"

They settled on a park bench under
a tree, its wide umbrella-arms
thick with leaves that made
a deep pool of shade.

"You speak to God in countless
ways," the father said.
"Today you heard many people
speaking to God."

He put his arm around her, and she leaned against him.

"What do these people say when they talk to God?" the girl asked her father.

"They say, 'I love you,' "
the father answered.

"I didn't hear them say that."

"There are other ways
to say 'I love you' to God
without using just those words,"
he said. "Think about what
you have heard people say today.
Think about it and remember."

The girl thought. She remembered
the laughter, the song,
the kindness, the love she had
heard people give to each other;
and she smiled at her father,
because she understood.

The father said, "I love you,"
and she snuggled against
his warm chest and answered,
"I love you too." And she
knew this was a way
of speaking to God.